A COMMONPLACE BOOK

A *Commonplace* Book

poems

by

H. A. Maxson

Published by **BLAST PRESS**
324B Matawan Avenue
Cliffwood, NJ 07721
(732) 970-8409
gregglory.com/blastpress

"...what thou seeist, write in a book..."

— *"Revelations"* I. ii

"The work in process becomes the poet's fate and determines his psychic development. It is not Goethe who creates Faust, but Faust which creates Goethe."

— *Carl Jung*

"For the creative order, which is an extension of life, is not an elaboration of the established, but a movement beyond the established, or at the least a reorganization of it and often of elements not included in it."

— *Brewster Ghiselin*

"Darwin's notebooks lie at the tail end of a long and fruitful tradition that peaked in the Enlightenment-era Europe, particularly England: the practice of maintaining a 'commonplace' book. The great minds of the period...were zealous believers in the memory-enhancing powers of the commonplace book. In its most customary form, 'commonplacing' involved transcribing interesting or inspirational passages from one's reading, assembling a personalized encyclopedia of quotations..."

— *Steven Johnson*

Contents

Tracks 15

Threshold 21

Revelation I 23

"Revelation" VI 23

Revelation II 24

"The Snow Begins" 27

Word Storm 29

Vatic Voice 31

Evanescence 32

Prayer 33

Negative Capability 34

Islands 36

The Posture of Seekers 37

Dahlias 38

Dog Death 1956 39

Migrations 41

Swarm 42

Canadas 43

Snows 44

The Horses 45

An Aubade 46

Dream Dissolving on a Morning 47

Petit's Air 49

Fossils 51

Gardens 53

Setting Out Seed 54

Blue Doom 55

On the Last Total Supermoon Lunar Eclipse
    of my Lifetime 56

The Sky is 58

Meditation on a line by Loren Eiseley 60

Sandy Hook : A Quartet 61

Things I Should Know and Don't 66

A Poem by Mr. Mark Twain found in his book
    Following the Equator: A Journey Around
    the World with Over 190 Illustrations 68

Travel 69

Caribbean Dreamin'* 70

Caribbean Dreamin' II 71

Hearing in Tongues 72

"Another Part of the Island" 74

Altos de Chevon 75

Birds: Playa Del Carmen 76

Pareidolia 77

Moc: Rite of Passage 84

Organized Violence 87
Stone and Wood 89
Two Paintings 91
Conch Tanka 93
Spring Worms 94
Art 95
Silhouettes 97

For Maureen

Tracks

"Half a billion years ago a creature slithered across the sea floor for the first time. It may have launched an evolutionary arms race."

—*Rob Moor*

I. Shot Hole Borers

Look close, here, here and here they entered
the pulpy underworld beneath bark,
through bore-holes round as shot, round and spaced
as any planned invasion. And then they tunnel—
but aimlessly—perhaps in search of something
we can't know—their loops and straight lines, their crooked
trails and cul de sacs—they might be deer paths,
native trails, or timbered-out pioneer roads
through Kentucky's of new land.
                                        They show us...what?
they gave up and died, or doubled back
following their own scent of frass, or the familiar
   groove they cut through pulpwood: what? A day, a week,

a month ago? I found quartered log
after split log full of them. Bark on
I would have missed them; stripped they are
pure Pollocks.

II.

Or obscure maps:
deer runs, native paths, the chaotic
cross-hatchings of Colonial mud roads—
perhaps they resemble cloverleafs,
bypasses and highway exits seen from heaven,
a rabbit warren only the rabbits can navigate.
Who can guess the system of yields and stops?
Maybe there are laws even beneath bark,
stops, turns, reverses give us little to go on.
We have just the maps, not the destinations;
we have roads or rail beds, not the locomotion.
We track without compass or constellation,
We are clear-eyed observers above,
mole-eyed below.

III.

In the chaos of firewood—cut, split
and dumped in the yard, are many maps
of discovery, the unknown
(*there be monsters!*), invasions or escapes.
They are chock-a-block with information
for those who can read them, for those with no
rosetta stone: confusion heaped on chaos.

IV. Ediacarans

How like the Precambrian ediacaran's

soft-bodied tracks, left by those blind vegetable-

animals that heaved themselves over sea bottom

six hundred million years ago—plant-animals—

sacks of mud, someone called them--that learned to flop

and slide, wriggle, plod, slither awkwardly

from one world into the next and leave a few texts

for us to read of that transition from leaves

or fronds awakened into animal dreams of slime—

passages mindlessly followed—to leaving

footprints, tracks, trails unclear messages

as to who they were and where and how they went—

no hint about the long, slow limp to the beaches

up into the trees, down onto savannahs,

and finally here to the nib of a pen speculating

origins of everything gilled or lunged today.

V.

Slower—much slower—than second hands
the first mobile ediacarans
humped over slime beds nutrient rich
and green. We cannot imagine the slow heave
 of time over slime on muscles just emerged
from... what? Plant roots, fibers shocked
or tickled to grope or glide?
If the still ones
had eyes, what would they have made
of a neighbor, a frond, no less, inching away
from the stationary tribe—centimeters a day
or week, waving a paddle-shaped leaf
as if to say goodbye to all of that.

Threshold

"It was really a very little episode, and if it hadn't been for the squirrel I wouldn't have seen it at all. The thing was: he stopped to think."

—*Loren Eiseley*

Last evening's gray squirrel studied
dried corn I tossed into the yard.
Too large to carry, he nibbled it
on the open lawn, but grackles and red-wing
blackbirds bedeviled him with their comings
and goings.
                    I watched him rise
on his haunches and study the yellow cob.
He tried once, twice, three times to lift the ear.
When he dropped it, it rolled. He rose again
to contemplate, took the silk end in his mouth
and pulled, gained a few inches, but it was yards
to safety under the cedar trees. He sat.

This afternoon, loading the wheelbarrow

with firewood, I find the cleaned, red-brown cob

between two stacks of oak. I congratulate us

for wood and corn that will warm us one more night.

Revelation I

Two for my grandfather W.F.M.

(1) "And I saw when the Lamb opened on of the seals, and I heard, as it were the noise of thunder, one of the four beasts saying 'Come and see'...(2) And I saw and behold a white horse...(4) And there went out another horse that was red...(5) And when he had opened the third seal...And I beheld, and lo a black horse...(7-8) And when he had opened the fourth seal...I looked and behold a pale horse..."

"Revelation" VI

I never noticed them before, the tic marks

and pale, pencil underlines, parentheses yoking

verses in your Bible I somehow inherited.

Chapter 6 is nearly disassembled,

your farmer's eye drawn first

to *white horse*, then *horse that was red*

then *black horse* and *pale horse.*

Your deacon's eye to *peace* but not

crown instead *peace on earth*

not *power* or *sword* or *hunger*

but *beast* and *barley*

figs, and, oddly *white robes.*

Revelation II

"...there were voices and thunderings and lightnings..."
"Revelation" 8

The afternoon you died we freed limbs
brought down by storm, the worst
we'd seen in years. Standing soaked
on my father's deck, he strained
to hear my mother's words, small
and damped down by thunder.
It was dark and my father seemed to flicker
from the lightning in the southern sky.
I searched his face for news as rain
sluiced down his face and hair.
We went back to work, but without
his zeal. Later, dry in the house,
he said you died at the moment
of the thunder that shook down
the limbs.

In your *Bible*, twenty
years later, I find in "Revelation"
8, the only phrase you underlined:
thunderings and lightnings.

"The Snow Begins"

Outside the snow begins.
Inside "The Snow Begins"
hangs on my office wall.

I watch the year's first snowfall—
wispy as spider webs,
the threads warp and weave,

knit the air into patterns of *leave
and wander, love and go home.*
Outside the snow begins.

Inside "The Snow Begins,"
by William Carlos Williams
hangs on my office wall

but this comes gently over all,
he writes, *all crevices are covered...
wounds are healed*

white, white, white as death.

Outside the snow begins.

Inside, "The Snow Begins."

Word Storm

"Through the fence, between the curling flower spaces, I could see them hitting. They were coming toward where the flag was and I went along the fence. Luster was hunting in the grass by the flower tree. They took the flag out and they were hitting. Then they put the flag back and they went to the table, and he hit and the other hit. Then they went on…"

— *William Faulkner*

I dreamed last night of words,
                         broken words;
words of runes and letters; words that could not
be said in a kaleidoscopic landscape, a bombed out
neighborhood blasted to just edges and corners
with a soundtrack of croaks and gibberish;
word pieces littered the dream, a junkyard
of words and word parts;
                       words spun like windsocks
in a gale of blather; it was a feverscape, but this time
a loop of word scraps and tatters where voices stuttered
and went silent; after the maelstrom of cracked, chipped,
splintered, dented and mangled letters—letters rendered

in Coptic and Cyrillic and cryptic—I remember thinking
that this place is where poems come to die.

Vatic Voice

"We are passive to the vatic voice, as the cloud or the tree is passive to the wind."
    —Donald Hall

I am driving and writing a poem
about drought in my head.
Write what you know, they say,
and I am making a list of all
the driest words I know:
barren, arid, parched, juiceless.

A ticking begins and at first
I think I must have driven through
a swarm of bees. But it's rain,
strange stuff in a summer of drought
and heatwaves tailgating heatwaves.
Even though the windshield is wet,
it doesn't fully register. It must be
some minor god, I decide,
speaking in tongues.

Evanescence

"Everything that happens in this world is an expression of the intentions of an intelligence superior to us…"
    —*Sigmund Freud*

Out of sleep we drag

the dust of dreams

the crumbs of nightmares.

We disappear. We return.

Mornings we half remember

the remains of a night—

but they're the only proof we have

of where we've been.

Prayer

"*"Young gardeners were busy on their knees preparing for spring."*

—*Maribel Osler*

All of this kneeling

to weed, kneeling

to plant

        is prayer

and nothing less.

Negative Capability

"*"I mean Negative Capability, that is, when a man is capable of being in uncertainties, mysteries, doubts, without any irritable reaching after fact and reason —"*

—*John Keats*

Some say the soul weighs 21 milliliters,
escapes the body at death and leaves
it lighter:
            what then does an idea weigh?
A memory? A notion? A thought? Hope?
Does a nightmare outweigh a dream?
What about a belief or a philosophy?
Would any of them balance a scale
with a soul?
                What if I don't lose my soul
at death, just my mind? What does *it* weigh?
And while I'm asking, where does it live?
And what do halations weigh, the give
and take of life, expansion and contraction?
Or a heartbeat itself? Not the heart, or blood,

but the pulse—does it weigh the same as a blink?

A twitch? An ache or pain? What tips it

joy or sadness?

Islands

"For the islands I sing/and for a few friends;/not to foster means/or be midwife to ends."

— *George Mackay Brown*

Islands forever rearrange themselves,
their hooks, coves, bights and points
shift or disappear, rise and fall becoming
islands forever rearranging themselves.
Sand wanders. Rocks, shells, the odd
remains of life meander the shape-shifting
islands. We forever rearrange ourselves,
our hooks, coves, bights and points.

The Posture of Seekers

"Now and then a stooping figure moved in the gloom or a rain squall swept past me...there was a faint sense of coming light...soon I began to make out objects, up-ended timbers, conch shells, sea wrack..."

    —*Loren Eiseley*

Hunched, they walk the tideline,

eyes fixed on the ridge of waste

the tide brings.

                Stooped, they pluck

some treasures glinting, a gift

among dead and ruined things—

a whole shell or a polished pebble—

something else to lose or misplace

along the crooked tideline of days.

Dahlias

"The transforming force of gardens is undeniable. Not what we do to gardens, but what they do to us."
    —*Mirabel Osler*

I remember the dahlias, taller than a boy,
a jungle of them in our yard with blooms
larger than a dinner plate, and colors
now seen only in dreams. I hid among
the stalks, thick as a man's wrist.

My father would trade the bulbs
with Sammy Bolton who lived up the hill
and cultivated dahlias like my father—
a pale orchid purple would come down
the hill and a pumpkin colored one go up.

In the fall the bulbs were dug and grouped
by shades in old peach and bushel baskets
and sent to the cellar to winter and where I
would go daily just to smell the earth
they brought with them into the house.

Dog Death 1956

I.

Because tonight our black lab slipped
her wet muzzle under my hand that half slept
on the sofa arm, I wake to a dog I never knew.

Where my wife sleeps a few feet away, was yard
when we bought this house, was where
Russel's dog lived in its house sixty years ago.

"After Russel died," my neighbor told me
years ago, "his widow kept the dog
chained, right about where your bedroom is."

II.

For months wasps must have built their nest
inside the dog house where dog and bees coexisted
until one day the arrangement soured.

"He was chained on a ten foot tether, wasps
one day got pissed off and attacked, stung him
over and over and over—about the middle of your room."

Migrations

"The explosion of farms and farmland caused an explosion in the grackle population."
    —*Bird Migrations*

This morning is busy with grackles.
And loud.
    The trees fill
and then the air with the iridescent
flicker of wings.
    All day
like breath they will go out
and return—some god's halation
of delight
    until some distraction
and they are gone—south—
until their onemind sends them back.

Swarm

"The most exciting movement in nature is not progress, advance, but expansion and contraction, the opening and shutting of the eye, the hand, the heart, the mind."
—*Robert Frost*

Today midges swarmed as I walked
the dogs to the pen. They hung, pulsing
four-five feet in front of me.
When I moved, they scattered, the cloud
shattering into shards that beat.
I stopped. They formed a ghost,
over and over, like breaths in winter.

Again and again dispersal
and coalescence—dilation and contraction.
Then tonight, fog particles, smaller than midges,
gathering, swarming the porch light.

Canadas

"How do geese know when to fly to the sun? Who tells them the seasons? How do we, humans know when to move on? As with the migrant birds, so surely with us, there is a voice within if only we would listen to it, that tells us certainly when to go forth into the unknown."

    —*Elisabeth Kubler-Ross*

Geese are on the wing this morning.

First light and wave upon wave of voices

low and loud as whispers on water

weave earth and air and waves together.

Mist rises above old snow drifts, a shroud

that billows and ripples on goose noise

(too staccato for song). In the field

something hunkers February bright

and moves slowly off toward the treeline.

In here we gather our day around us

take what we need out into goose voice

and snow melt. But first, in the corner

we watch a moth blink awake

in a pale pale haft of sun.

Snows

"What man-made machine will ever achieve the complete perfection of even the goose's wing?"
  —*Abbas ibn Firnas*

I thought it was a field of snow
where no snow had fallen—
or a trick of light that happens
now and then on days like this—
fair in mid-February and sun
coming at a steep pitch across the field.

But it was geese wing to wing,
settled into drifts, or settling,
chevrons exploded into squalls.
I have seen whole tidal marshes
ripple like snow in wind
with their white anxiety.

The Horses

"It is a commonplace of all religious thought, even the most primitive, that the man seeking visions and insight must go apart from his fellows and live for a time in the wilderness. If he is of the proper sort, he will return with a message. It may not be the message from the god he set out to seek, but even if he has failed in that particular, he will have had a vision or seen a marvel, and these are always worth listening to and thinking about."

— *Loren Eiseley*

I used to watch the horses reconstitute

themselves in the fields early mornings

out of mist or fog more dense

than any winter breath. They emerged

hoof to pastern, fetlock to cannon to knees,

hock visible, gaskin blooming, then flank

and withers and poll. Complete. A polaroid.

And they stood chewing, as nonchalant

as party guests, bored and unimpressed

with the morning's miracle.

An Aubade

"Most things will never happen: this one will."
    —*Philip Larkin*

A dog voice scores the morning,

slips in under sleep

and scripts a dream.

I take a long time waking,

the comedy gathering in blind fits.

And suddenly it is all bird song

and wind in the trees,

palaver of early mornings

and the waking to

and not merely a waking from.

Dream Dissolving on a Morning

"And truly I was afraid. I was most afraid, but even so honored still more/that he should seek my hospitality/from out the dark door of the secret earth."

—*D.H. Lawrence*

I have to make it up to make it real—
or most of it, some was coiled and waiting for me.
I recognize the Mississippi landscape.
I haven't lived there in two decades
but the landscape lives—the Red Headed
Woodpecker and the Pileated in the magnolia
I spent too many hours staring at as I mindtraveled.
 And there are the armadillos stealing cat food.
And there are snakes:
      Garter, Corn, Rat,
Milk and Coral, Pigmy rattlers, Copperheads
and Cottonmouths.
      I am balling something
in my hands—meat or potatoes or bread.

Beyond the window are pond, brush, trees, tall grasses.
It is all sky and small water in the distance
until I turn and there is some gray dream-
snake, purple-eyed, coiled and waiting.

Petit's Air

"Petit did not just walk the rope. He jumped, he floated, he ran back and forth, he joked."
    —*Arresting Officer, World Trade Center 8/7/74*

I remember a grainy newspaper

black and white of a quarter century ago.

Phillipe Petit on a thumb-thick wire

strung between the unfinished

World Trade Center towers—

nothing but a balancing pole between him

and the street a thousand feet below.

I remember the feeling: my feet sweating,

something slithering up my spine,

a fear of heights, even someone else's heights.

Today on the radio news they say there's a new movie

about that walk across big air, and it starts again,

my sweating—hands, feet, forehead damp,

the thrill up my spine to where I stiffen,

shift in my seat, the image of a fall that didn't happen

flashing in my mind. Then the voice of Petit
remembering that sixty minute ballet back and forth,
just out of reach. I wobble thinking about it,
a fear of heights, even someone else's.

Fossils

"Tiny tubes and filaments in some Canadian rock appear to be the oldest known fossils."

—*Malcom Ritter*

I am a finder and keeper of fossils,
they sit in shoe boxes in the shed,
decorate the tables on the deck, the railings—
shell impressions, and worms pressed into mud,
sand, magma. There are ferns in the slate
stepping stone in the garden. On a beach
of the Bohemia River I found a volcanic cup
my wife might plant violets in.
                    I keep spear points,
chipping tools and arrowheads. My notebooks
contain the fossils of failed poems. The English language
harbors fossils—*men, women, children*—the rest of their ilk
killed off by William Caxton when he set up his printing
press in London, not Oxford. In the basement family room

is an old TV, rabbit ears and manual dials.

It pulls in twothree local stations on calm clear nights, but mostly there's static—like fossils of the Big Bang.

Gardens

"…scanning a catalogue and knowing little, names are often the first thing to catch the imagination, long before logic."

—*Mirabel Osler*

Gardens begin long before

they are planted—in dreams

of orderly rows of starter leaves,

thick stems and flawless fruit;

in late spring, old nightmares

of green chaos, the anarchy

of fickle harvests.

Setting Out Seed

"I never saw a wild thing sorry for itself."
—D. H. Lawrence

This is the season of hunger:
of thaw and bud, first twigs
and dry grass shaping into nests,
of too few worms
rising to rain, or flies
and midges rousing from torpor.

Despite our diligence of seed,
cracked corn, suet, tithe of stale bread,
they are hungry,
they harrow the scavenged ground,
they glean the barren places.

Blue Doom

"Years ago I planted 'loosestrife'—just for its name—and have been distraught ever since."
—*Mirabel Osler*

Pretty, we said, when we planted the corner,
put in a border of heather, planted wispy
grasses and three or four stones for accent.
Pretty, we said the following spring
when the pale Blue Dune emerged early
before we'd cleared away last year's tangle
of growth. *Pretty soon*, we said, that blue stuff
will take over the garden. Its rhizomes invade
the heather and blue leaves poke up everywhere.
Pretty damn stupid, we said pulling every leaf
and root we could find tunneling up from hell.

On the Last Total Supermoon Lunar Eclipse of my Lifetime

"It will be the first 'supermoon' lunar eclipse since 1982 and there won't be another until 2033."
   —Daily Mail.com

No more will monsters eat the moon—
never again in my sight will god
palm the full moon like a stage coin
and make it vanish.
                    No more
will the night's bright eye blink;
for the last time we have celebrated
the strange emergence of the moon
from mere halo. No dragons will inhale
dark's brightest cinder, or the sky
serpent strangle the last light
or demons steal the doubloon of night.
It is done:

all of the myths, magic, speculations,

the thefts and inhalations, strangulations

of lunar light:

the moon will stay put until I'm finished here.

The Sky is

"…contrails…force lines on nature, which knows no lines."
—Peter Tyson

carved with minims—
gray slashes, old runes
or a new alphabet
printed on the morning.

II.

Sonic plowshares
ripping the sky
to furrows.

III.

This morning's slashes and grids
are the tacit agreement that lines
and crosshatches equal meaning:

so we say, so we agree:

the sky is sermon; the sky is report;

the sky is us and not us;

the sky is minims, runes, furrows,

and some say message.

Meditation on a line by Loren Eiseley

There was a meaning...
The way the light hit the leaves—
I thought it was raining.
Light does that sometimes,
leaves too in this season—
and there was not a meaning...

The sun was dimming, but still playing
cat and mouse behind late afternoon
clouds. The maples have gone mostly brown
only hints and whispers of color
this drought year
                      and therein lay the agony.

Sandy Hook : A Quartet

"Then last of all, caught from these shores, this hill
Of you O tides, the mystic human meaning:
Only by law of you, your swell and ebb, enclosing me the same
The brain that shapes, the voice that chants this song."
  — *Walt Whitman*

I.

It was quiet my first hour here, only the sailors
out early in Sunfish, Day Sailers and catamarans.
Then the outboards came, skimming like flat stones
across slate-grey water. On the other side of the bight,
where the bay becomes river, the party boats loaded.
Now the water shakes, forms into waves and rumbles
shoreward. It is audible jetsam. It is flashy, cheap
effluvia that drowns silence and the thoughts
that whisper through the silence. That quiet
must disturb many, they work so hard, here on the bay,
to kill it like an unknown creature that surfaces

dumb, blind and hideous in its unfamiliarity, and must die because of its otherness and because it would be harder work to try to understand the other.

II.

Though I have listened to the sound
of Atlantic waves breaking for nearly
three decades, I still stop and behold
the varieties of pitch and sizzle and rumble,
the variations in the surge, sway, overpitch
and swash dissolving into hardpack second
upon second upon second. And there is the stutter
of rhythm, not the regular pulse or beat of music,
but the infinitely different. There is a sameness,
of course, a debt in each voice to some perfect wave,
but no two I have heard sounded the same.
Like snowflakes, fingerprints, or pearls
each borrows an elemental shape or cadence
or voice from all that came before, but each exacts
its own change, exacts an alteration that cannot
be repeated—plays once and is gone.

III.

The bay was flat again, gone silent.
For hours there was only the clacking
of shells making into a ridge at the apex
of tide. That and the wish-wish of bay
scrubbing the sand. A few gulls,
half a dozen fish crows, two terns
and a red-wing blackbird rummaging
the landscape for a meal as noon simmered
toward 90. A few hours of that kind of silence
and order grows in importance in direct
proportion to the bedlam of dead and cast off things.

IV.

For an hour I watched a horseshoe crab,
blind and mindless creature, stall
at the shoreline, half in half out
of the swash. Small brain or instinct
utterly stopped him. The warmth of sand,
the cool of ocean merged in dark confusion
washing him gently : *go to the light*
and warmth after the cold rebuke of winter.
Stay, to leave means endless circling sand
in search of the sea that's receded in your drowse.
I did not wait for his decision. I moved once
to take him by the tail and fling him back
into deep water. But I didn't. His order is not mine,
nor mine his. I truly fear sometimes that such a random act
might disturb some order or balance so fine
that my life might stagger with the consequences.

Things I Should Know and Don't

"...not till we are completely lost, or turned round—for a man needs only to be turned round once with his eyes shut in this world to be lost—do we appreciate the vastness and strangeness of nature. Every man has to learn the points of compass again as often as he awakes, whether from sleep or any abstraction. Not till we are lost, in other words not till we have lost the world, do we begin to find ourselves, and realize where we are and the infinite extent of our relations."

—*H. D. Thoreau*

I wish I'd learned the stars better,
the fanciful human and animal shapes
some folks can effortlessly point out
to those challenged, like me.
                                        I wish
I'd learned more trees than just the ones
in my lifetime of backyards, and the birds
by their songs, the flowers by their scent.
God knows I've had enough time to close
my eyes and recognize my favorite apples

by taste, the pears and citrus by scent.

I almost know the wood I burn,

the cut of a steak, the varieties of tomatoes.

Almost. I sniff the wine in restaurants

(but not at home), swish and pretend,

but all I really know is wine from vinegar,

a taste I like from one I don't.

I know a red from a white with my eyes closed,

but the stars, trees, flowers, birdsong...

A Poem by Mr. Mark Twain found in his book Following the Equator: A Journey Around the World with Over 190 Illustrations

"...None of the idols in Banares are handsome
or attractive. And what a swarm of them there is!
The town is a vast museum of idols—
and all of them crude, misshapen and ugly.
They flock through one's dreams at night,
a wild mob of nightmares.
                                        When you get tired
of them in the temples and take a trip
on the river, you find idol giants, flashily painted,
stretched out side by side on the shore.
And apparently wherever there is room
for one more lingam, a lingam is there."

Travel

"Allons! The road is before us!...Let the paper remain on
the desk unwritten, and the book on the shelf unopened."
  — *Walt Whitman*

What sits on my desk—a nineteenth century
library table, one central drawer, book shelves
on both sides—on less space than a sheet of paper
is a cell phone, a short wave radio,
a digital recorder, and new polarized sun glasses.
None of these existed in my youth,
some not in middle age.

They all live in little black bags. They all pop to life
with one touch, respond to voice, or eye or ear.
I pick up my globe the size of an orange
and trace my trajectory south two weeks from today,
a white island on a blue ball, Republica Dominicana.
When I was ten I filled a canteen
and bicycled to the other end of town—
when the other end of town was the exotic.

Caribbean Dreamin'*

The seven sisters of the pliades glimmer
up there somewhere between midnight and infinity.
I step out into the cold moonless night—
the seven sisters of the pliades glimmer—
and watch a shaft of contrail arc south
its arrowhead blinking a morse code goodbye
up there somewhere between midnight and infinity
while the seven sisters of the pliades glimmer.

*Lines from Jimmy Buffett *A Pirate Looks at Fifty*

Caribbean Dreamin' II

If there is a heaven for me,
I am sure there is a beach attached to it.
Jesus is the answer, but the question was
if there was a heaven for me.
I was born with salt water in my veins,
sand is my marrow, seaweed my soul.
If there is a heaven for me,
I'm sure there's a beach attached to it.

Hearing in Tongues

"From this hour I ordain myself loos'd/ of limits and imaginary lines…"
    — *Walt Whitman*

I listen, listen. I don't understand,
but I listen. I cannot name the tongue,
the many tongues that I listen to,
but for a little while each night
I dial in the world's cacophony,
close my eyes and ride the cadences,
the occasional meters, the points
and counterpoints that speak
beyond the words to meaning other,
other than the dry denotations,
even subtle connotations to common
rhythms of the blood, the drum
of the heart, translated into pulse
and breath and the blink of an eye.
I ride a human voice
to Timbuktu, to Sao Paulo,

to Kinshasa or Beijing.

For a moment I tumble on a burst
of breath formed and shaped
and blown across the globe.
I listen, listen. I understand,
and I listen—hard.

"Another Part of the Island"

"It is better to travel well than to arrive."
   —*Buddha*

Over there was just far enough away
to cloud certainty. There seemed
to be a house—a building, at least—
and north of that a bridge,
more north a beach where tiny
figures appeared from time
to time. And south of the beach,
but north of the uncertain house...

But that's all the evidence we could gather,
that and the catamarans that set out
each morning, and the dolphins
that animated the blue middle
distance, and the point break
and the dark flats that all gave
the eye a moment between here
and the lush green uncertainty
of over there.

Altos de Chevon

"We remember a flange of the sea, deep/ Mountains, and
one of those cameos/ That slip into your life sometimes…"
  — *William Stafford*

For weeks I have tried to remember
the name of the river we floated
while eating lunch, and the modern
village high up on a limestone cliff,
and the amphitheater built
to look ancient, Roman maybe,
but a long way from the empire—
New world, Dominican Republic—
a ribbon of river below us
bending, brown in contrast to
the impossible green of its banks.
I stood a long time today
watching the river, and cliffs float
their memories over a still and quiet
place in my mind where a name should have been.

Birds: Playa Del Carmen

"A delirium of birds."
— *Theodore Roethke*

The flamingoes won't cooperate,

won't herd, puddle or say cheese.

They gather in a pink huddle.

They are an alphabet of necks,

a runic pink chaos of legs.

By the time I focus, they are cryptic.

"Stay," I whisper, but their pink disorder

dilates and contracts, melts and jells

and I aim into a tree and shoot a toucan.

Pareidolia

"...a psychological phenomenon in which we see familiar shapes where none exist."

—*National Geographic, February 2017*

I.

Summer days in the bronze-grass meadow over Johnson's

hill that no one seemed to know but us, we saw wheelbarrows

and fat men, steamships, bicycles; the ferocious eyes

of a cat stared down before dissolving like a dream.

Clouds were shape-shifters we'd always been told;

above that field they shaped stories as clear and strange as myth.

II.

At night we learned to connect the dots the stars arranged

at distances we thought were myths themselves: Archers

and dogs, twins, bulls, scorpions and crosses we could and could not

see even as we squinted, shifted north to south, west to east,

then settled on Sirius, Pollux or Betelgeuse, the single lights

that required neither astronomer nor poet.

III.

From time to time I read pseudo-scientific reports
of ink or blood stains the perfect image of Jesus or Mary.
I supposed elsewhere in the world they would see Buddha
or Zarathustra smiling from a dried puddle of coffee
or tea on last Thursday's newspaper or a notebook page;
a grease stain from taco, egg roll or fish and chips.

IV.

Decades ago, in Sunday School, they gave us

a photograph of melting patches of snow.

They told us that true believers could see the face

of Jesus in the chiaroscuro Rorschach landscape blotches.

I was desperate. I lied that could see the eyes,

nose, a mouth, long hair, then worried I might burn forever

for that unforgivable Baptist prevarication.

V.

Our discussion cannot ignore appearances
of holy and profane visages in slices of toast
or pizza cheese, pie crust or artisan bread.
We see. We behold. We witness. We proclaim
that we see what others see; we participate in mass
hysterics and we are welcomed into benign self deception.
We hold hands and hug and weep and pray.

VI.

I have spent as much time indoors as out, staring
at tile and tree bark, carpets, and undergrowth.
I have found Lincoln lurking in unexpected places,
women costumed from other centuries, children,
animals, runes and letters revealed on a walk
or a glance at the floor. I never feel alone
in the woods or my living room.

VII.

Skiagraphs are another thing, they're images
that appear in heartwood—portraits and bestiaries,
flowers and horses fixed for decades if not hundreds
of years. No imagination needed. No denial accepted.
Precisely where the chainsaw opened the log
(a half inch off either way—no picture) a tea kettle.
No guess work, just a gift from Fra Pandolf's storied hand.

Moc: Rite of Passage

"Do not disturb or attempt to handle! Its bite is far more severe than that of the Copperhead and can be fatal."
—*Audubon Field Guide to N.A. Reptiles and Amphibians.*

I.

It was almost a dream.
We had all caught garter and black snakes,
kept them a day or two then let them go
into the tall grass in Morris Walsh's field—
home too to epic battles and box turtles.
Today, for no good reason, I remember
a snake coiled and thick-bodied as a boy's arm
and hundreds of miles north of where it should
have been. But suddenly there it was (and is again)
on the tramped-earth path around Navesink pond.

Three boys, we studied to memorize
the patterned skin that coiled in serrated
bands from tail to its spear-point head.

We, the snake and the day were quiet.

We ran home and looked it up in *Americana*: Cottonmouth; Water Moccasin; Snap Jaw.

We closed the book, warned of its fatal bite and short temper, but we returned armed with sticks.

II.

Over half a century later I feel
the weight of challenge, not to touch the death
that could strike at any moment, but to simply
jump over it, to leap the snake and hope
it did not waken.
                      We argued to be first,
but my neighbor simply launched himself over,
stood smiling on the other side of the Swamp Lion
basking a few feet from the water's edge.
The dark back and paler belly were still
a rounded puddle of snake unaware
of our gawking as it slept. My brother jumped
next, one moment beside me, the next over
there, bent in half as if he might be sick.
I was the last. Fat kid, I grew heavier
by the moment. I rocked back and forth,
bent my legs—"if I should die…"—
I did not. And that Water Pilot drowsed
in the August sun over 60 years ago.

Organized Violence

"Poetry is organized violence upon language."
    —Robert Frost

Driving to teach literature to Airmen,

I hear on NPR of young vandals who drank beer,

broke furniture then pissed and spit on artwork

in a farmhouse in New Hampshire.

And not just any ramshackle or abandoned farmhouse,

but the Frost Place, summer home for fifty years.

Two dozen caught and punished, punished by the house's

former owner, convicted to sit and hear about the man

they'd wronged, then hear his words in "Out,Out."

Jay Parini said they were not prepared, these vandal-
    children,

for the severed hand in the poem, the death in the poem,

they did not know, he said, that poetry is not flowers

and rainbows, and they sat stunned when the boy,

their age, dies, and the family, not dead, returns

to their affairs, as we, non-vandals, turn to ours

after an evening of poetry, "organized violence

upon language," as Frost once defined his work, peaceful, a story for the ages.

Stone and Wood

"Stone, tree, star, fish, animal, man/ All gathered/ Within one circle of light and fire."

    —*George Mackay Brown*

And then there are the old collaborations
 of man and stone, of man and wood:
walls and fences, wells and bridges,
foundations, roads and walks, caves
castles and cities. What isn't
built of, in or on them?

Consider cairns, pyramids, cobbled streets,
Roman roads and aqueducts, Stonehenge,
Mo'ai of the Rapa Nui, basalt Olmec heads.
In the Yucatan alone there are uncounted
cities buried, waiting the machete to release them
from the obscurity of time and jungle.

Consider all that's lost to termites and water,
rubble in the wake of storm and sand and wind:

from posts decayed in earth we build fancies
in the air, from tumbledown rock we build
what we dream was or could have been.

Much we revere is stone, much we fancy was wood.

Two Paintings

—*Time* Photographs, Valazquez and Cotan April 28, 2008

Cave dark and history deep,
the blackness heaves these subjects
into relief—woman and boy,
cabbage and melon and quince.

They seem to emerge, whole
and complete—the white
of an egg is whiter than white,
the old woman beyond age,

the boy, ageless—holding the pumpkin
of youth and the flagon
he may succumb to—staring
into a past or a future.

Her face is a photograph
of resignation, the boy's a study

of contempt. They are caught

forever between hunger and contentment,

Between the blackness they emerge from,

And the light we view them from

and the posed middle ground

they will inhabit—forever.

Conch Tanka

"a still small voice…"
       —*I "Kings" ixx*

A whisper in a shell:
music, white noise, some god's small
voice like swash slipping
into sand? Listen. Listen:
it's the tide of your own blood.

Spring Worms

"So with animals, some spring from parent animals according to their kind, whilst others grow spontaneously and not from kindred stock; and of these instances of spontaneous generation some come from putrefying earth or vegetable matter…"
    —*Aristotle*

I pinch chickweed and dandelion,
vetch and popseed out by the roots
and worms percolate from the soil.

No wonder the ancients believed
life sprang spontaneous from earth
and river ooze—
               they sprout, sinuous
and the color of bruises.

No wonder when my shovel slices them
in two they writhe and coil and heal
casual as cloud and river.

Art

"Homespun, handmade, and quirky (as far from the strict artisan's guilds and trained masters of Europe as you can get)."

— *"The Story of Tramp Art…"*

This shelf, inherited from my grandparents,
is hobo art from the 20's or 30's carved by a man
out of work, hungry man who could whittle
for a meal something useful out of cast off wood.

I run my finger over the honey patina,
I imagine him shaping this in his mind.
Blade to whetstone I see him planning
Two, maybe three, steps ahead, for whimsy
half moons, an apple here, a pineapple there—
symbol of friendship he thinks—
he takes handsful of sand and rubs the wood
  until the grain is smooth as the cotton of my
grandmother's apron.

                        He passes to her hand

two hours of work as greens and ham hocks
are passed to him, down on his luck
and just passing through.

Silhouettes

"...a la silhouette was a reduction to the simplest form."
— *"Silhouettes by Hand"*

For years my brother's silhouette and mine—
nibbled from black paper on the boardwalk
in Atlantic City, hung on my parents' bedroom
wall—one of us staring east, the other west.

By the time they came down, his pug nose
was in the grave, and mine grown old.
Like the dressers, highboys, night stands
and closets full of clothes the profiles
went ingloriously to trash.

My grandparents had them too in a sunless
hallway between bedrooms, our black stares
gathered dust then went cheap at auction
or garage sales, gone like our heights recorded
in the kitchen doorway buried now
under a stranger's paint.

About the Author

H. A. Maxson is the author of 18 books—6 collections of poetry (*Turning the Wood, Walker in the Storm, The Curley Poems, Hook, Lemon Light* and *Grasmere)*; a book-length poem (*The Walking Tour: Alexander Wilson in America*) and a novel in free verse (*Brother Wolf*); two novels (*The Younger* and *Comfort*—co-authored with Claudia H. Young); a study of Robert Frost's sonnets (*On the Sonnets of Robert Frost*), and seven works of historical fiction for young readers, co-authored with Claudia H. Young. Over 1000 poems, stories, reviews, essays and articles have appeared in periodicals, journals and anthologies. He has been nominated several times for Pushcart Prizes. He holds Ph.D. from the Center for Writers at the University of Southern Mississippi and has taught literature and creative writing for over four decades at the college level. Married to Maureen Maxson, a nurse and photographer, they are organic gardeners in Milford, DE.

About the Publisher

Meet Me in Botswana:
What is BLAST PRESS?

A speech for national poetry month about BLAST PRESS by Gregg Glory

Ab li dolen in l'air [look up: beauty falls from the air]
"A book should be a ball of light in your hands."
~~ Ezra Pound

  As we all know, April is "International Guitar Month." But my heart twangs for poetry, and I was invited here to tell you a little bit about a tiny poetry publishing company called **BLAST PRESS**.

  Let's start with what **BLAST PRESS** is not. **BLAST PRESS** is not a community. It is not a community-building venture. It is not by, about, or for "the people." Unlike the pretentious anthologies that weigh down university shelves and slander the individual by gluing him into some historian's scripted story, **BLAST PRESS** is not a collection of individual voices expressing the vibrancy, meaning, and tradition of the creative community—nor of any community. In this respect, **BLAST PRESS**, as its critics have bitterly asserted, is nothing at all.

BLAST PRESS has published over 100 chapbooks and softbacks by some thirty authors over the past quarter century. Each author's work stands singularly alone and apart. **BLAST PRESS** does not take part in the mish-mosh of the magazine market, where a hundred tentative voices are corralled by brute binding into an ersatz herd. We go alone, each of us, to where the crocs swim alertly in the bulrushes and the nights are long. Meet me in Botswana, if you will meet with me at all.

What is a chapbook? A chapbook is a saddle-stapled booklet of plain paper stock folded in half with a sheet of colored card stock for a cover. In the first decade, booklets would be stapled together by hand, each staple closed with a bloody fingertip to save the two-cent per staple cost. All small publishers are unified in this regard: we are exceedingly cheap.

In the next few minutes, for a brief moment, we will hear the voices of some poets that have been published by **BLAST PRESS**. Their words have been put into chapbooks with a **BLAST PRESS** logo on the back, and my current address somewhere inside the front flap. Words torn from the air and swatted into print. That is all. But, that is everything.

Author Ethos

BLAST PRESS is what I would call a "micro-publisher." We usually publish chapbooks—booklets under 100 pages in length. Our print runs are usually under 100 copies per edition. And **BLAST PRESS** has published over 100 chapbooks from some 20 authors in its career. The entire cost is assumed by **BLAST PRESS**, so we are the publisher, and not a vanity press or service.

BLAST PRESS has been sustaining its small operation—in the black, mind you, no small feat—for about 20 years now. We have had a few more ambitious titles where the book itself, the author, and **BLAST PRESS** decide to dedicate the extra resources needed to make the event a success.

Part of the **BLAST PRESS** ethos is to keep the authors in charge of their work so that they can maintain maximum control of their creative material in the out-lying years and don't need to be writing to **BLAST PRESS** for permission to re-publish snippets or poems.

BLAST PRESS catalog available at:
amazon.com/author/gregglory
and gregglory.com

Our Credo

Do not dispraise the light

That, singing whatever's brightest,

Undoes the theft of night—

—Touch to caress, or move to love,

As this thoughtless rhyme does prove.

From **Ascent**

A Solitary Headstone

Niggling addendum to "Meet me in Botswana"

Magazines, published with a week's, month's, quarter's or even a year's date grow elderly on the shelves in a way that a collection of one individual's work never can. What year does Shakespeare's book expire? Horace is renewed year by year, no matter how worn his saws may wane. But a magazine or casual collection of miscellaneous artifacts, no matter how august the individual members of the find, retain an interest for us mostly as a time capsule. Even the Egyptian tombs of the pharaohs hold more interest for us because of what they reveal about the era of their creation than for what they say about their putative occupants. Old poetry quarterlies are no different, although they may contain an Endymion.

This is why **BLAST PRESS** is dedicated to publishing single-author volumes and stand-alone essay collections almost exclusively. Unless a poet is unknown, there is no point in his publication being undertaken by a small press. And if an author is unknown, he is best presented to an unacquainted public in his own exclusive company. It is always wisest to let a guest unroll at least a few of his favorite tales before we escort him from the house. What is characteristic and worthwhile in the poet's voice will quietly assert itself over the course of his varied pieces much better than if we merely heard his alba or evensong in isolation, let alone in the cacophonous squawk of a miscellany. To the marriage of true minds, ours and the author's, let not serial publication admit impediments. Only appearing in magazines and periodicals is like never having a final resting place—a poet without a plot.

BLAST PRESS

324B Matawan Avenue

Cliffwood, NJ 07721

(732) 970-8409

gregglory.com

Also Available

Call It Sleep

H. A. Maxson

List Price: $7.75

5.06" x 7.81"

Black & White on Cream

106 pages

SBN-13: 978-0998482927
ISBN-10: 0998482927
BISAC: Poetry / American

About Call It Sleep

Call It Sleep contains a final section of poems about a son's experience of a father's illness and death. It give us a snapshot these events in a series of moments, from the onset of the illness to the final moment of death. The book is full of small and large acts of understanding, resonance and respect for one who has gone before. The book touches areas of feeling and experience that confront universal passages of living in a way only very fine poetry can do.

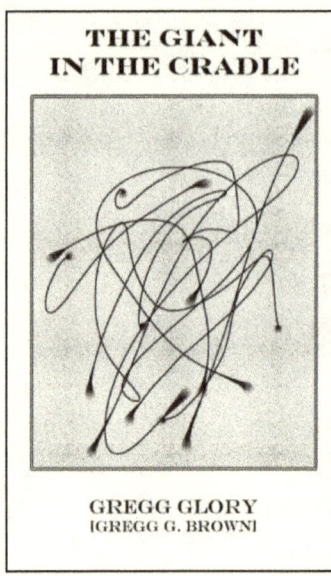

The Giant in the Cradle

Gregg Glory
[Gregg G. Brown]

List Price: $5.50

5.06" x 7.81"

Black & White on Cream

136 pages

ISBN-13: 978-1492396055
ISBN-10: 1492396052
BISAC: Poetry / American

FROM THE POEM "HEIGHT OF SUMMER"

Here is the day, the bridal day undaunted;
Here noon, at highest noon... hesitates...
The height of summer, at its crest arrested,
Held between warm hands to kiss—
The levitated real at pause in sun's perfection;
Paused because we cannot see, cannot imagine
Beyond such ripeness—

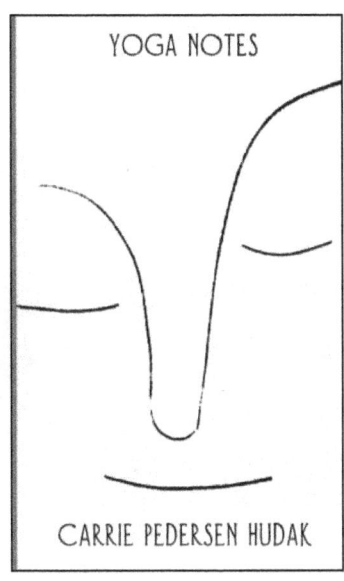

Yoga Notes

Carrie Pedersen Hudak

List Price: $5.50

5" x 8"

66 pages

ISBN-13: 978-1494330958
ISBN-10: 1494330954
BISAC: Body, Mind & Spirit

From the first essay: Just Practice

When I tell people I am a yoga teacher, they often say, I could never do yoga. I can't even touch my toes. Great, I say, you are already practicing awareness, that's part of the practice. Can you breathe? If you can breathe, then you can do yoga.

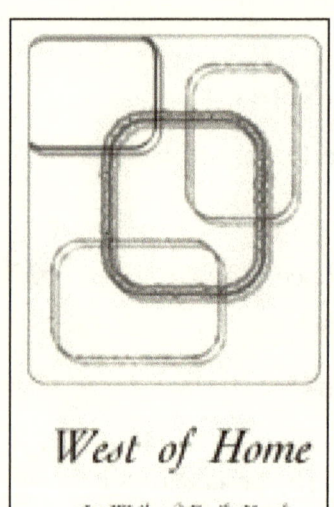

West of Home

Joe Weil, Emily Vogel

List Price: $10.00

Paperback: 98 pages

ISBN-10: 0615878415

ISBN-13:9780615878416

8 x 5 inches

From the Introduction

"West of Home" is a collaborative book of poetry which reflects the present and ongoing sentiments of Joe Weil and Emily Vogel. It includes 14 "responsorial" poems (call and response), between the two poets, as they respond to one another's themes and ideas, as well as two sections of poems, one for each poet's individual work.

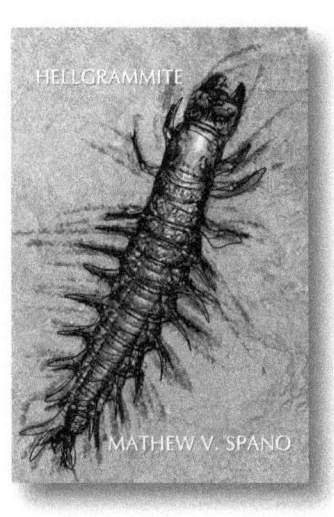

Hellgramite

Mathew V. Spano

List Price: $9.50

Paperback: 132 pages

ISBN-10: 0692761705

ISBN-13: 978-0692761700

5.5 x 8.5 inches

About Hellgramite

Hellgrammite" masquerades as a humble book of fishing poems and tales, but it is much more than that. It is a mythological multi-legged creature, creeping and crawling with vivid nature poems, ink drawings, sensitive haiku and two remarkably crafted short stories. By turns terrifying, tragic, witty and surreal, author Mathew V. Spano serves as the reader's guide, turning over river rocks of the unconscious and inviting readers to reach down into the wet darkness to probe mysteries of Mother Nature and human nature.

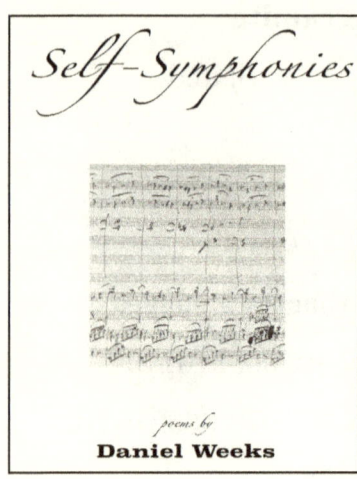

Self-Symponies

Daniel Weeks

List Price: $10.00

Paperback: 146 pages

ISBN-10: 0692238581

ISBN-13: 978-0692238585

7.4 x 9.7 inches

From the Introduction

Inspired by listening to the four symphonies of Johannes Brahms, Daniel Weeks's Self-Symphonies explore the landscapes, cityscapes, and seascapes that are the backdrop to a life lived on the New Jersey shore. The four long poems in this collection provide meditations on family, inheritance, and loss, society, nature, and culture, and stasis and change-- all of the elements that Coleridge said bething the individual self.

Bee Loud Glade

Authored by
Carrie Pedersen Hudak

Illustrated by
Nuria Tomas Mayolas

List Price: $11.99

Paperback: 36 pages

ISBN-10: 1548983217

ISBN-13: 9781548983215

8.5 x 8.5 inches

About the Bee Loud Glade

A letter from a young woman to her aunt considers printed books and social media.

The Pilot Light

Gregg Glory
[Gregg G. Brown]

List Price: $6.50

Paperback: 132 pages

ISBN-13: 9781511941921

5.5 x 8.5 inches

About *The Pilot Light*

The poems in Gregg Glory's The Pilot Light are about relationships—with family, friends, and lovers—along with reminiscences of a childhood spent close to nature in the New Jersey countryside. Glory is particularly adept at exploring the significant and oftentimes intimate moments that define our most important relationships, moments which, in turn, help us create the story of the self.

Knowing the Moment

Emanuel di Pasquale

List Price: $12.95

Paperback: 131 pages

ISBN-13: 9781503117471

5.5 x 8.5 inches

About *Knowing the Moment*

Emanuel di Pasquale has never been one to shy away from the more difficult aspects of living a full and engaged human life, and Knowing the Moment is perhaps his most searing work in this regard, as he confronts the hardships he encountered while growing up in his native Sicily. But these kinds of revelations are never the final word in his poetry. Tough times always seem to point him back to love—as he casts his mind back to life in Sicily or engages with the present in his poems about Long Branch, N.J.

Night, Night

Gregg Glory

[Gregg G. Brown]

List Price: $7.75

Paperback: 131 pages

ISBN: 1548801348

ISBN-13: 9781548801342

5.1 x 7.8 inches

From the introduction:

Entering a poem is like entering that other, underwater world. We are restored to a wholeness the pain of life and its deceptions has convinced us is missing. But, we can only hold our breaths so long before our imaginations burst! And still we go down like clockwork into the dark otherwhere of metaphor, easing past the shallow end of simile, our imaginations and lungs aching. However dangerous the journey, we will not be denied our diving, our entry into depths.

The Hummingbird's Apprentice

Gregg Glory

[Gregg G. Brown]

List Price: $5.50

Paperback: 159 pages

ISBN-10: 1511941928

ISBN-13: 9781511941921

5.1 x 7.8 inches

From *The Hummingbird's Apprentice*

ROADSIDE WINE

Pull off 71 suddenly, onto
a wide shoulder of dust and grass.
weigh down a length
of brown barbwire fence
like a wave of honey breaking.
Excited, splash ankle-deep
into the unhurrying surf
full of velvety bee sounds, and select
one perfect blossom. It is
so sweet in the slow afternoon.
And, where you've cut your thumb,
a thrill of air catches.

American Songbook

Gregg Glory

[Gregg G. Brown]

List Price: $3.75

Paperback: 98 pages

ISBN-10: 1482703297

ISBN-13: 9780692238585

5.5 x 8.5 inches

The Old Truculence

A note concerning the basic arc of this book of poems—to re-register grace and freedom as America's primary metier.

Freedom breeds elegance. Not the inbred elegance of aristocracy, where beautiful ladies eventually come to resemble their Russian wolfhounds. Nor, simply, the truculent elegance of that sly Benjamin Franklin who, as ambassador to the French Court, refused to bow before King Louis the 16th or doff his coonskin cap.

Freedom breeds the desire to create one meaningful action with your entire life—the effortful elegance of the artist that James Joyce defined as the willingness to gamble your whole life on the wrong idea, a bad aesthetic, or, it may be, a genuine triumph. And America has created, and can still create, a unique scale of opportunity for such elegant "throws of the dice," as Mallarme might say. A natty Fred Astaire (originally Austerlitz), gliding with the ease of an ice skater as he backs Rita Hayworth (a gal from Brooklyn) into immortality to a tune penned by the jewish Jerome Kern in an industry patented in the U.S.A. is but one example of the scale of that opportunity.

When you are free to do anything, a desire grows in the breast not to do just anything, but to do the best thing—and that is an aesthetic dilemma. The mere accumulation of capital, or the arbitrary exercise by minor government regulators of petty power, are two classic examples of the desire for a meaningful expression of life-status that lack the aesthetic instinct. Such timid ambitions grow most strongly where the full range of light is narrowed, and the blossom of selfhood must twist around corners to open its ruby glory in a thinning patch of sunlight.

Gregg Glory
March, 2013

Come, My Dreams

Come gather round me, multitudinous dreams

That in the dim twilight are murmuring soft;

Come lay by my head in the pillow-seam;

Come carry my freighted heart aloft.

O, I would dare dream as few men dream

Beyond the cruel cudgel of the strong,

Beyond the purpled tapestries of is and seems

Hung before my eyes, beyond cold right or wrong.

A BLAST PRESS BOOK

www.ingramcontent.com/pod-product-compliance
Lightning Source LLC
Chambersburg PA
CBHW031401040426
42444CB00005B/378